I0467768

ROW MAN SEA: Pure & Natural

Kevin Schnaubelt

ISBN:1500676659
ISBN-13:978-1500676650

I'M A STUDENT OF LIFES CONDITIONS:

Live and Love Life fully so that you may consider epistemology.

CONTENTS

	The Message	i
1	Clouds	1
2	Sun	4
3	Beach Combing	6
4	Sunset Colors	8
5	Sand	11
6	Flowers	14
7	Bridges	16
8	Trees	19
9	Boats	22
10	Critters	24

MEMORYS

Hope you enjoy the view from my path experiences.

CLOUDS

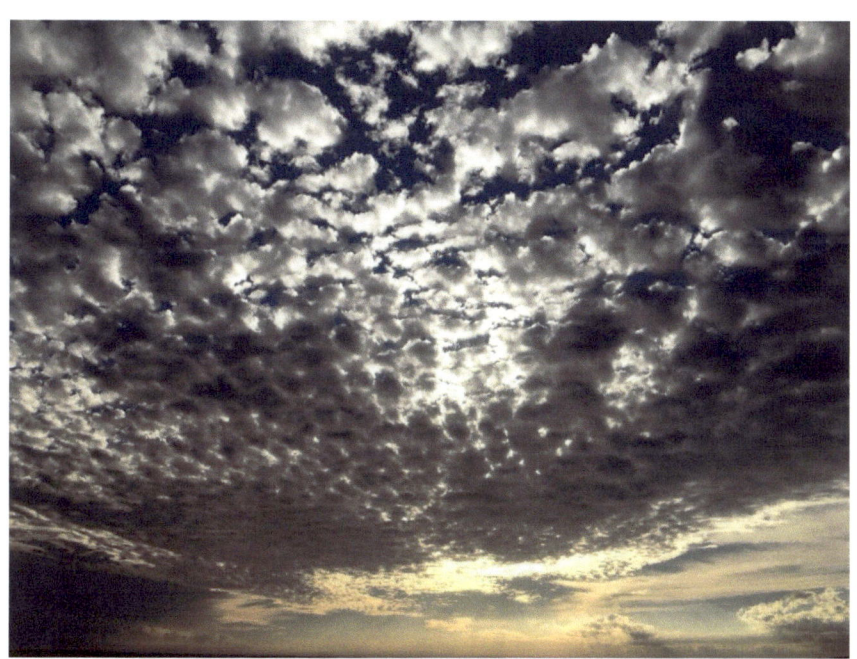

Popcorn Ceiling

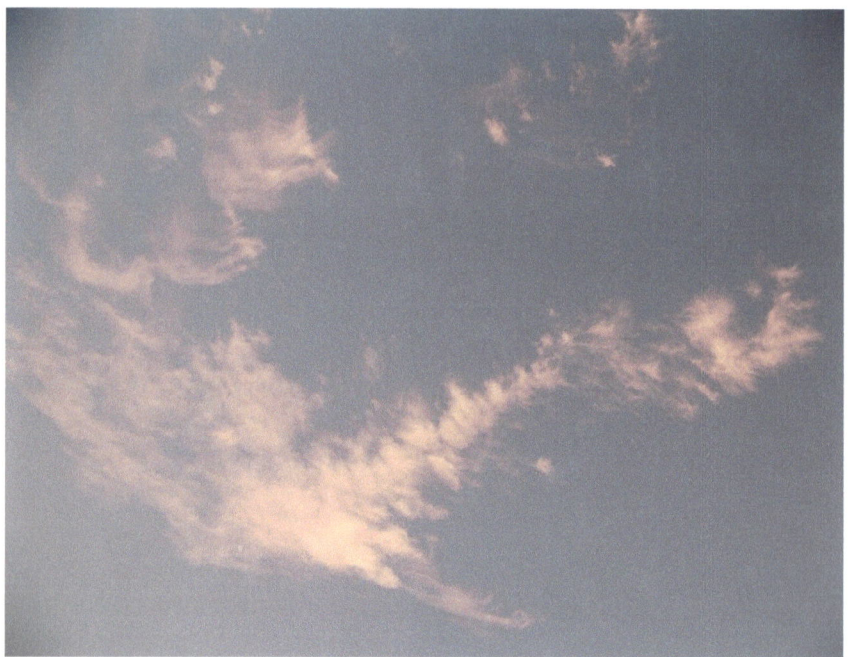

Casual Critter

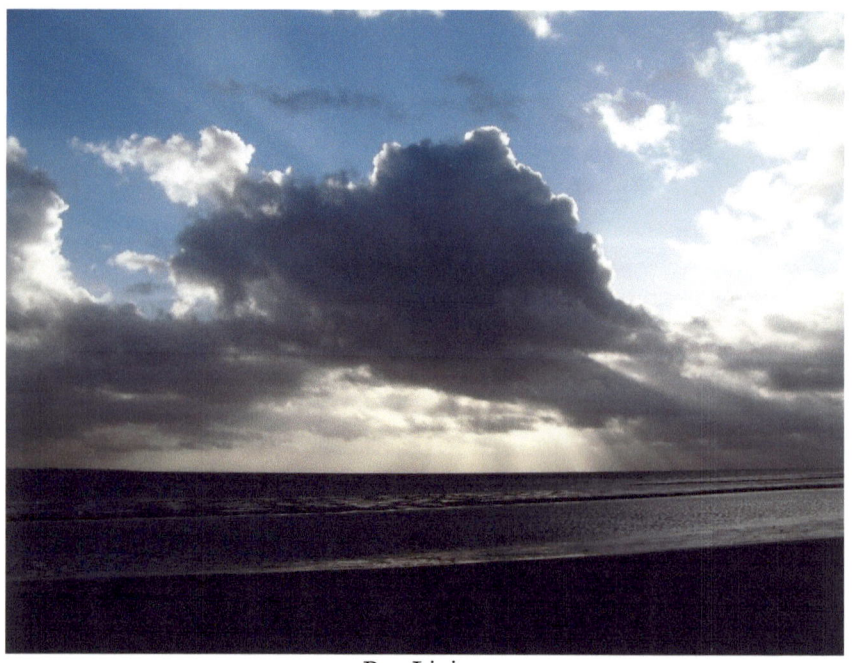

Ray Lining

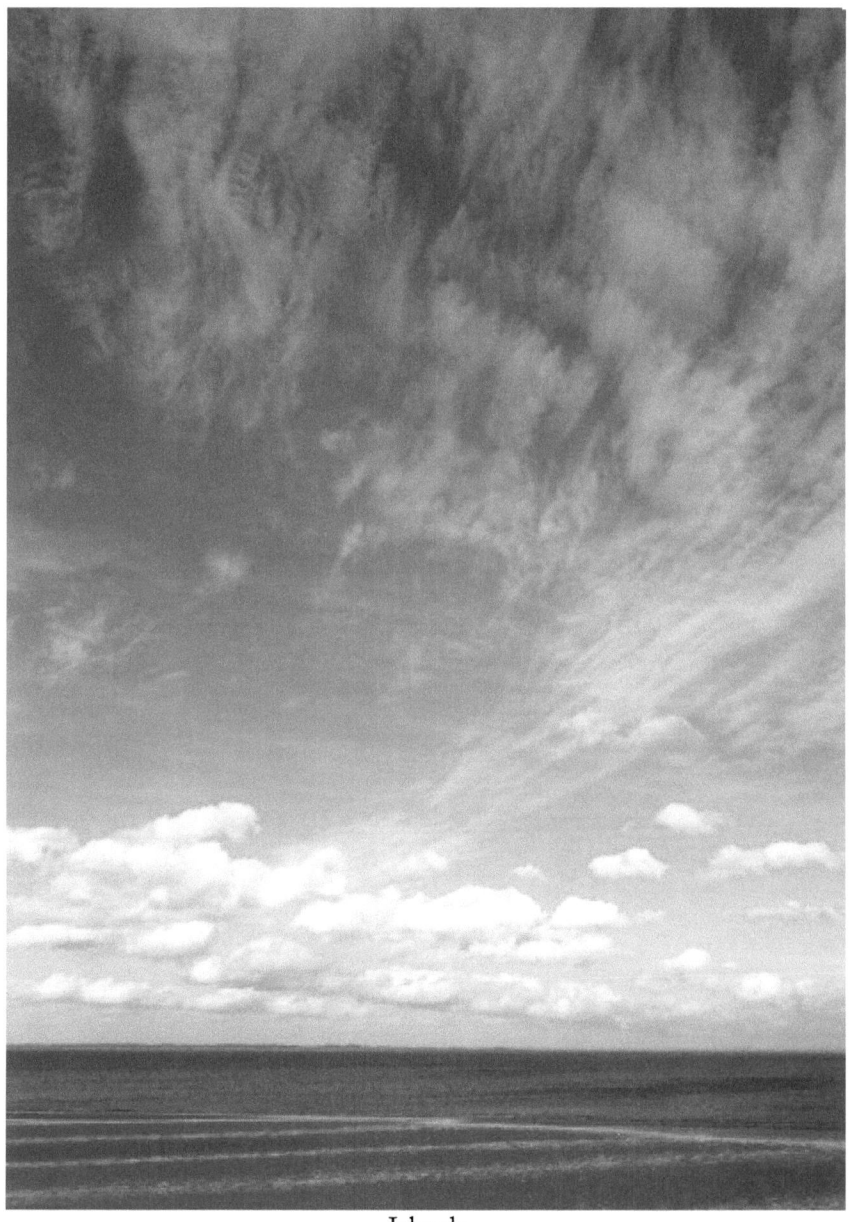

Islands

SUN

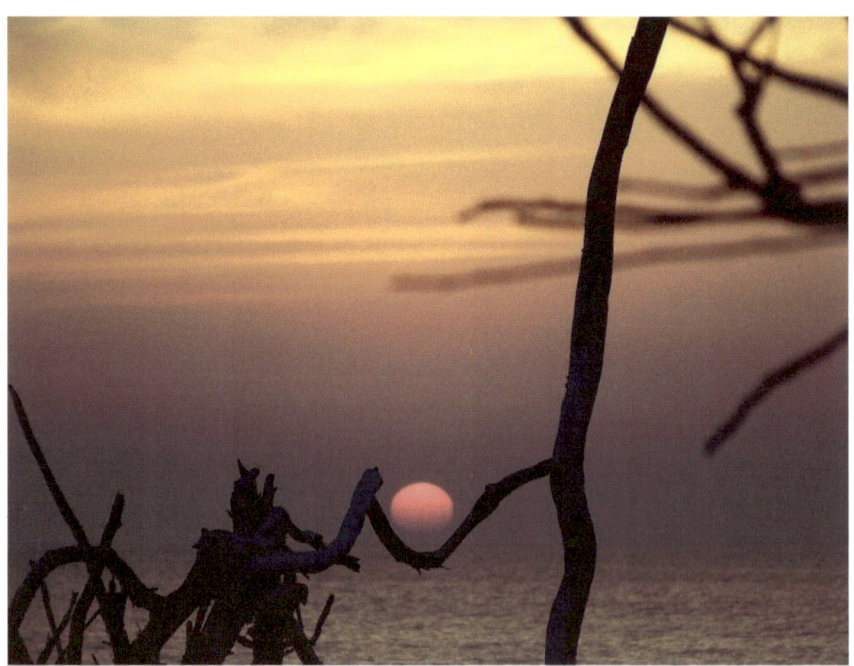

Embracing the Light

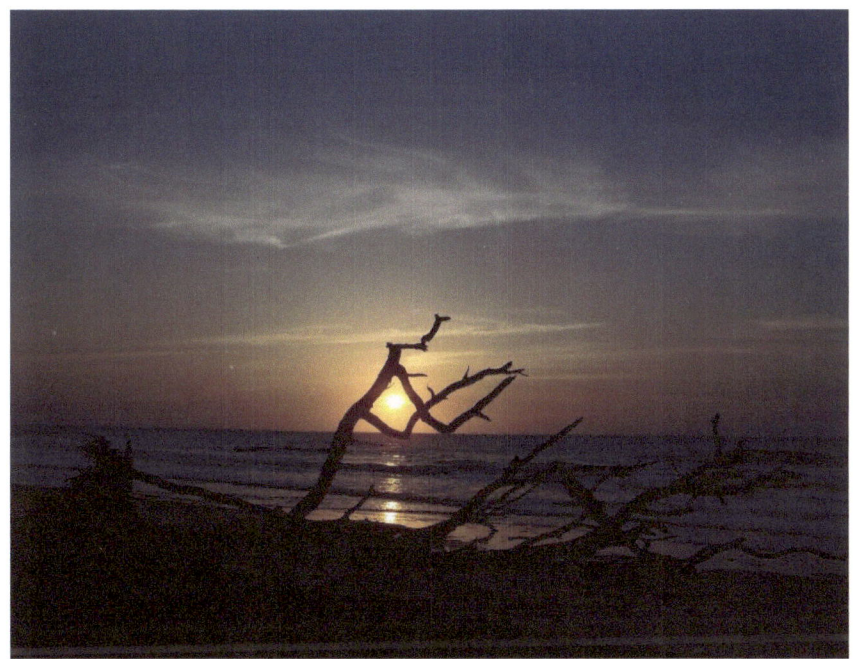

Praying Mantras

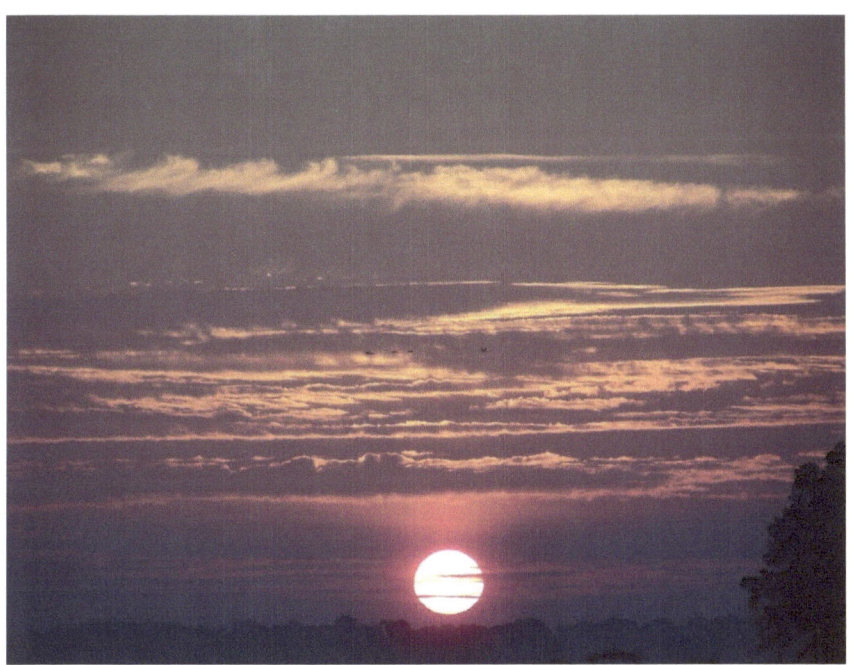

Pink Haze

BEACH COMBING

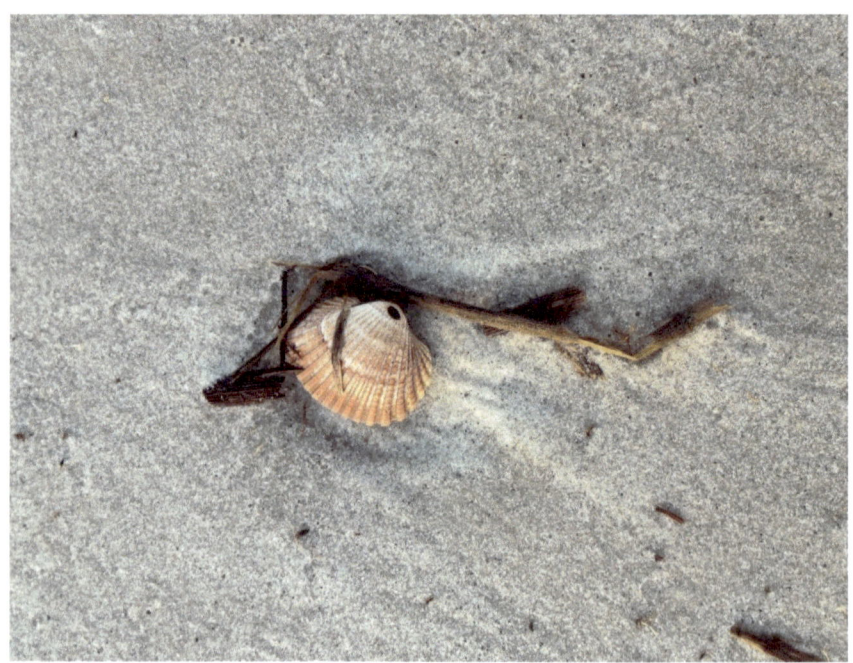

Shell Games

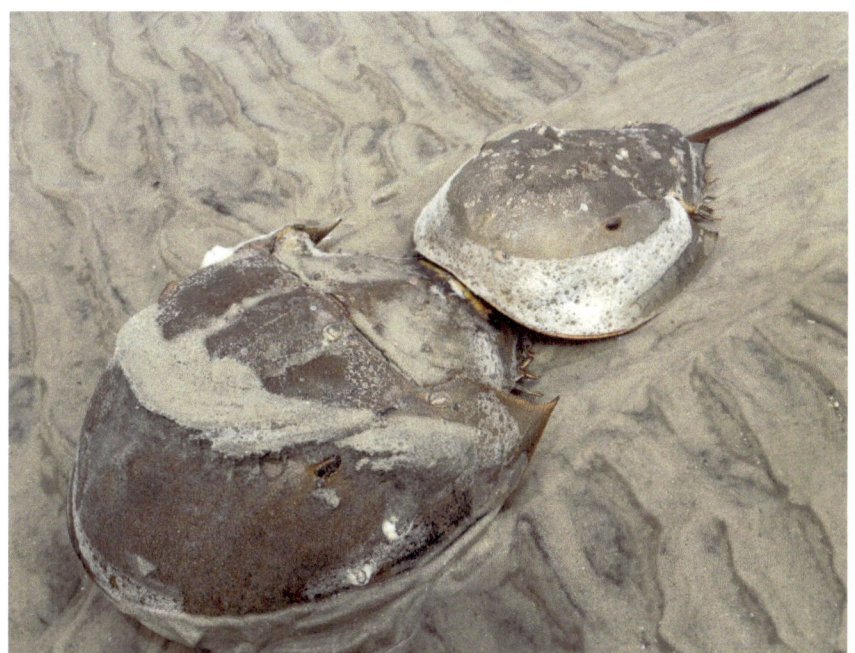

Crab Train

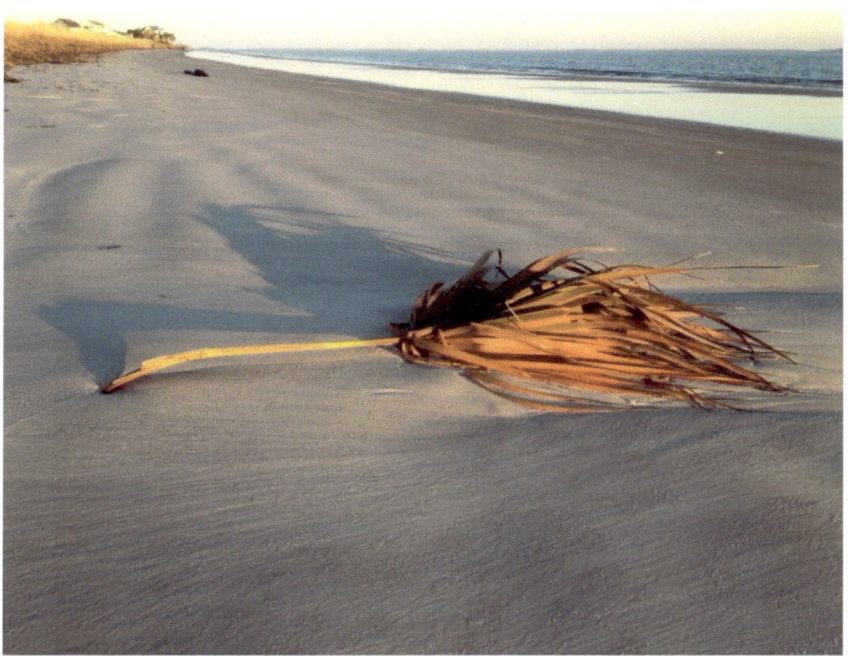

Palm Beach

SUNSET COLORS

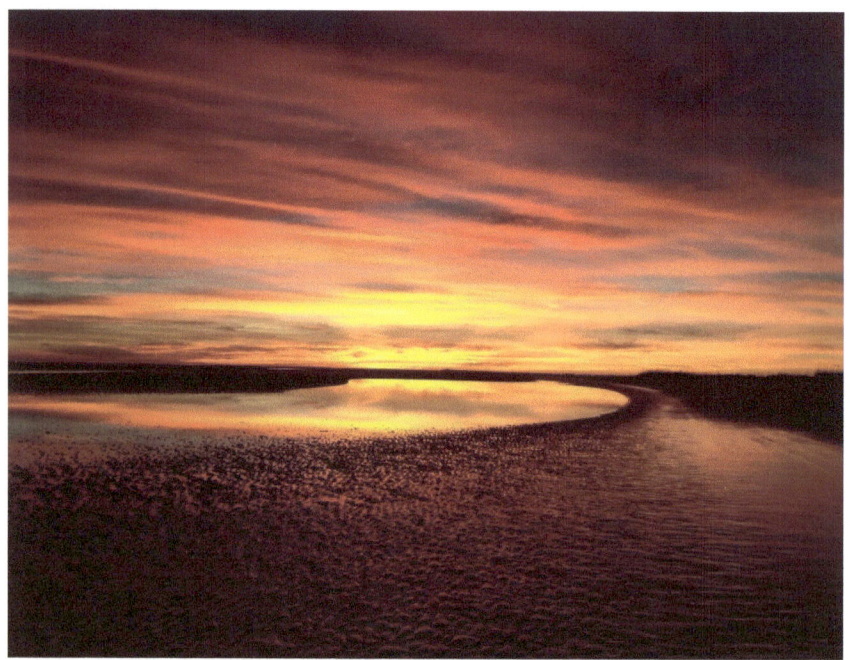

Translucent Creator

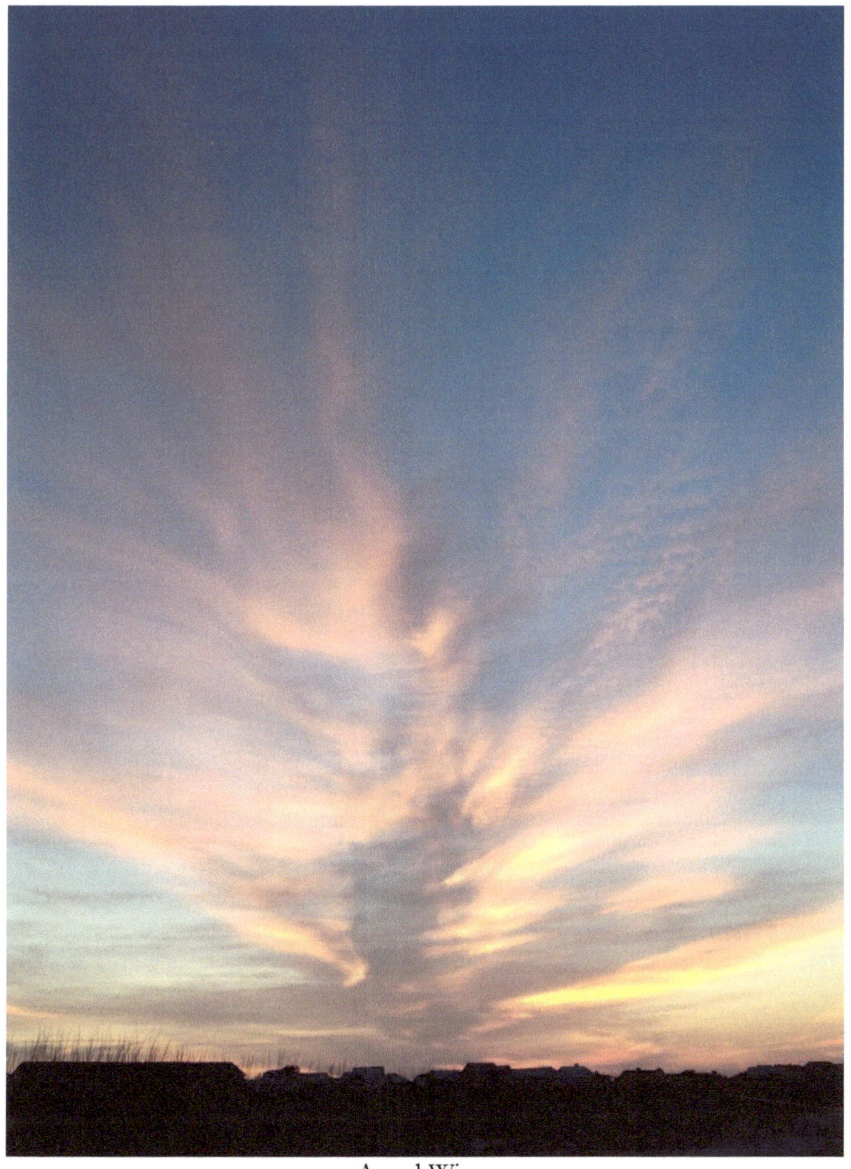

Angel Wings

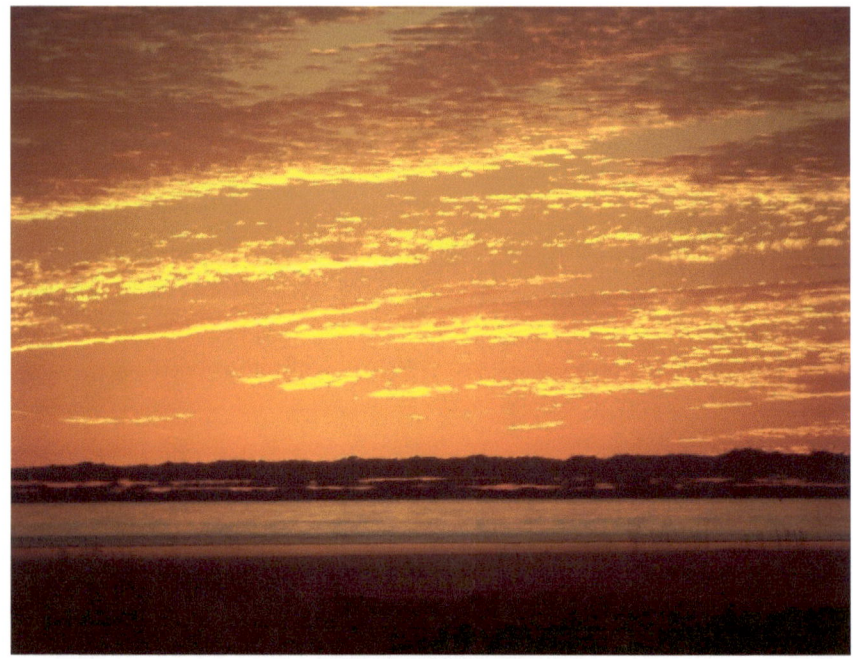

Blazing Horizon

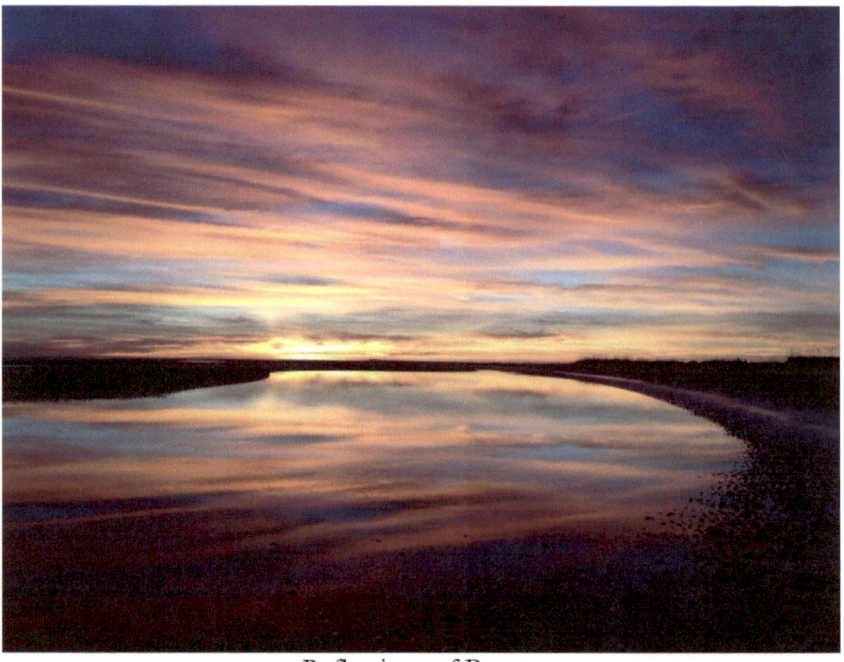

Reflections of Beauty

SAND

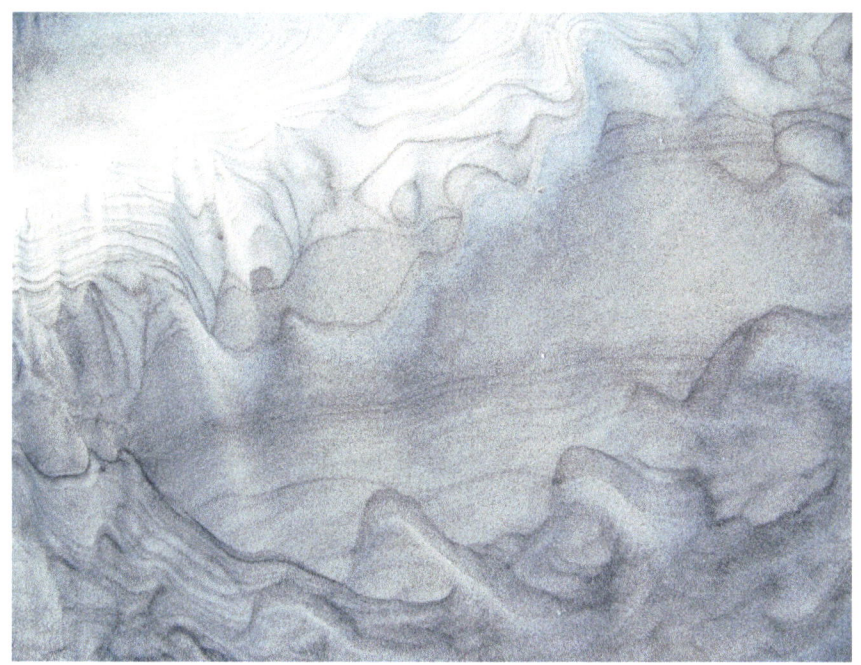

Natures Canvas

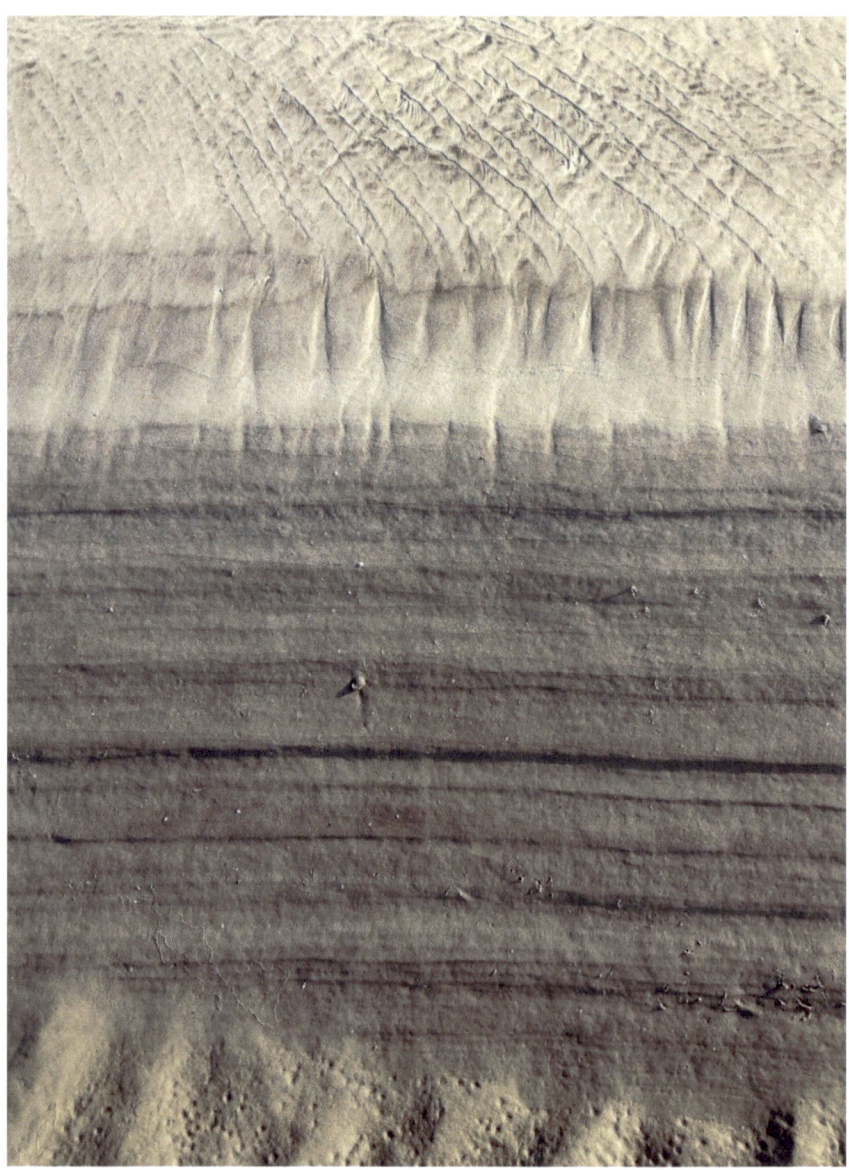

Cherokee Spirit

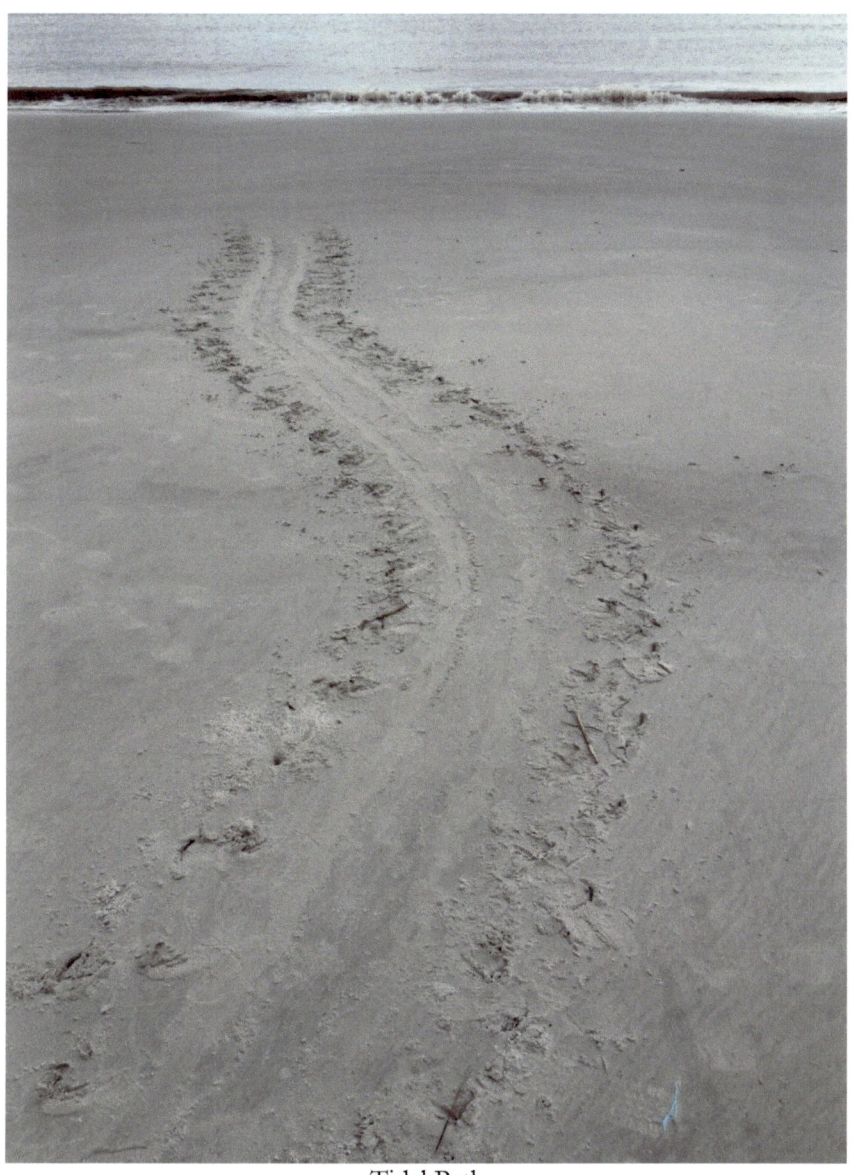

Tidal Path

FLOWERS

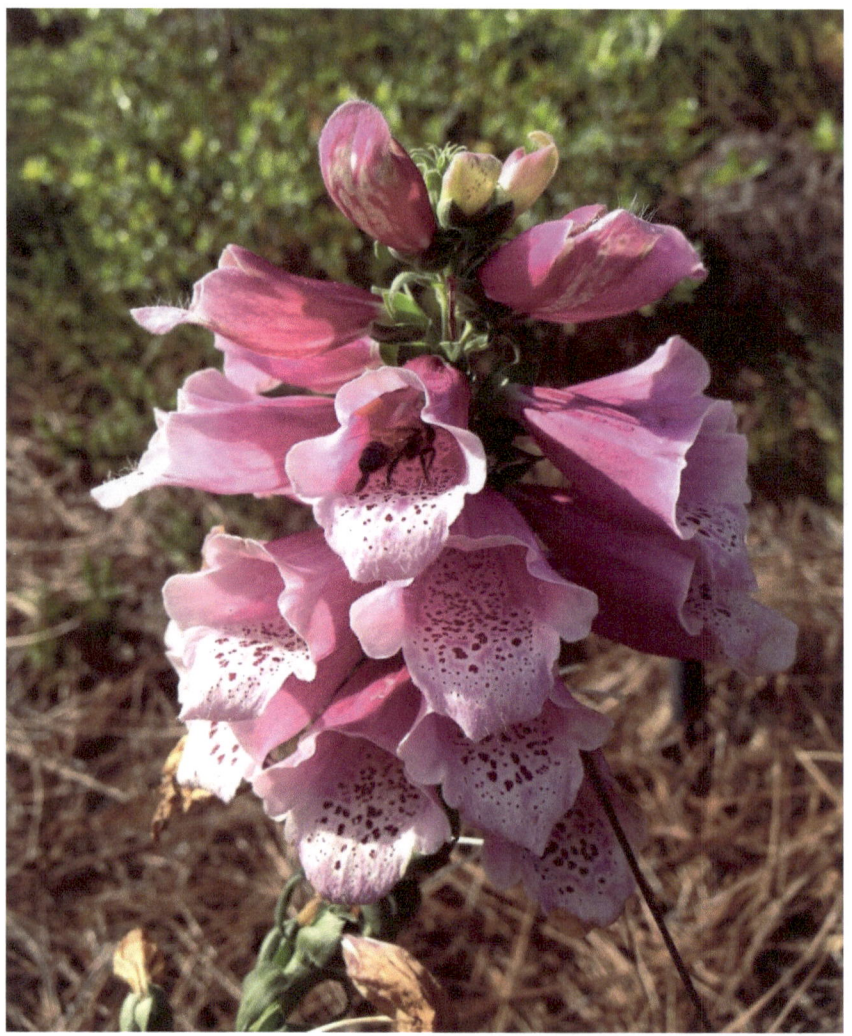

Pollen Count

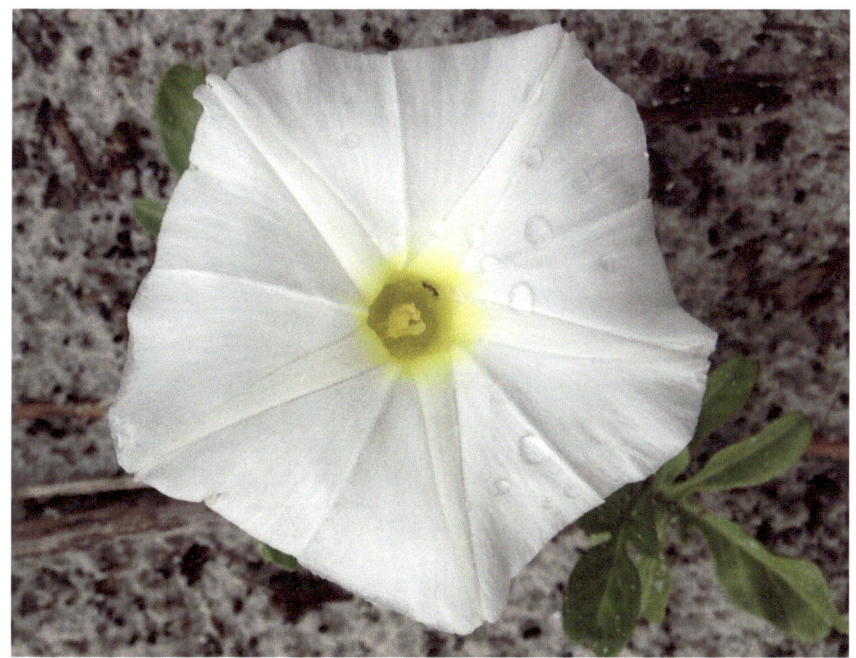

Aunt Rim

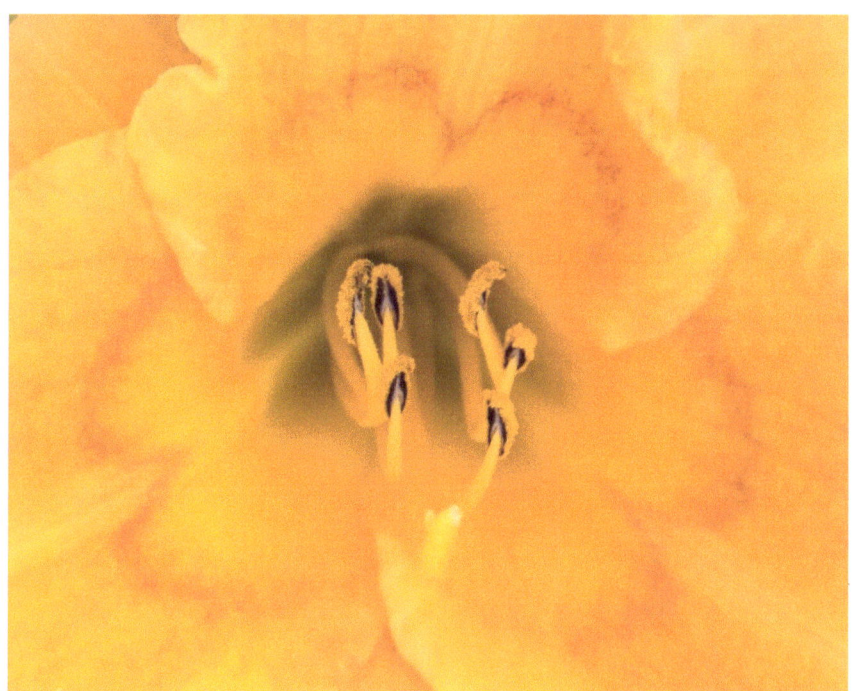

Glad Allover

BRIDGES

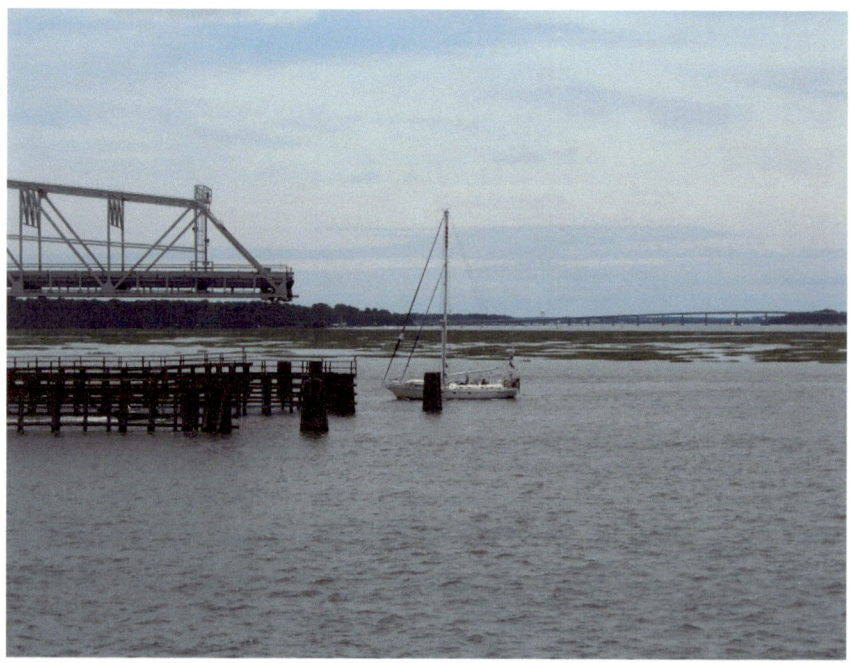

Water Landing

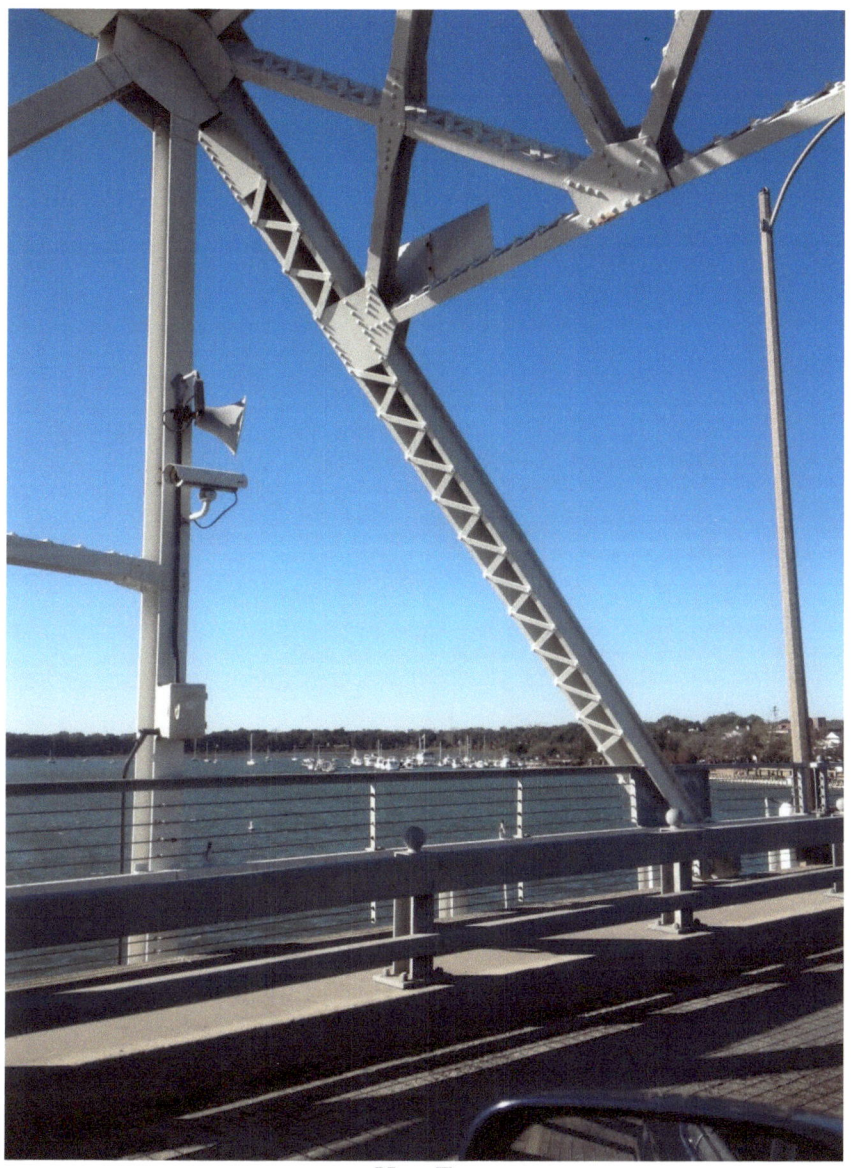

Hear Eye

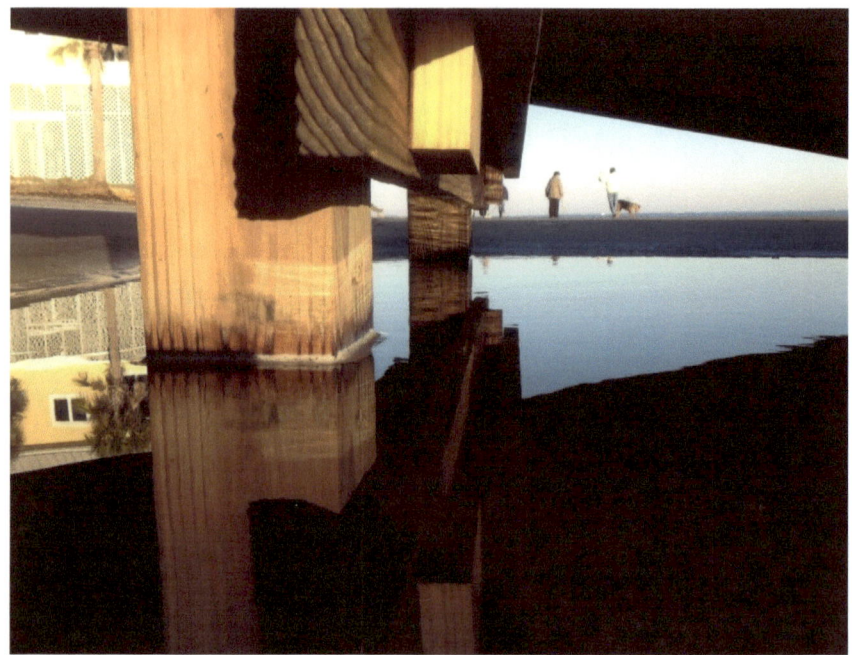

Under Over

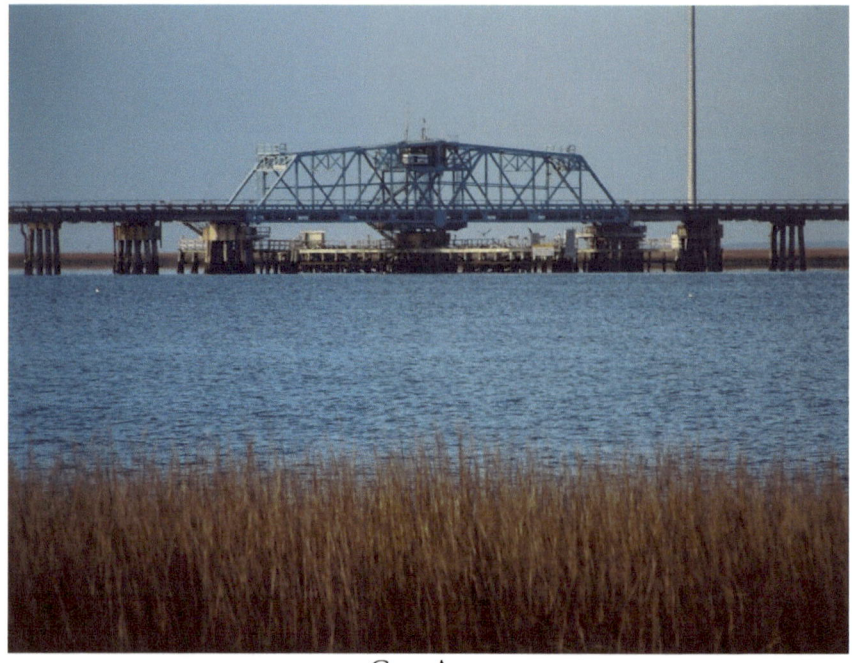

Gray Area

TREES

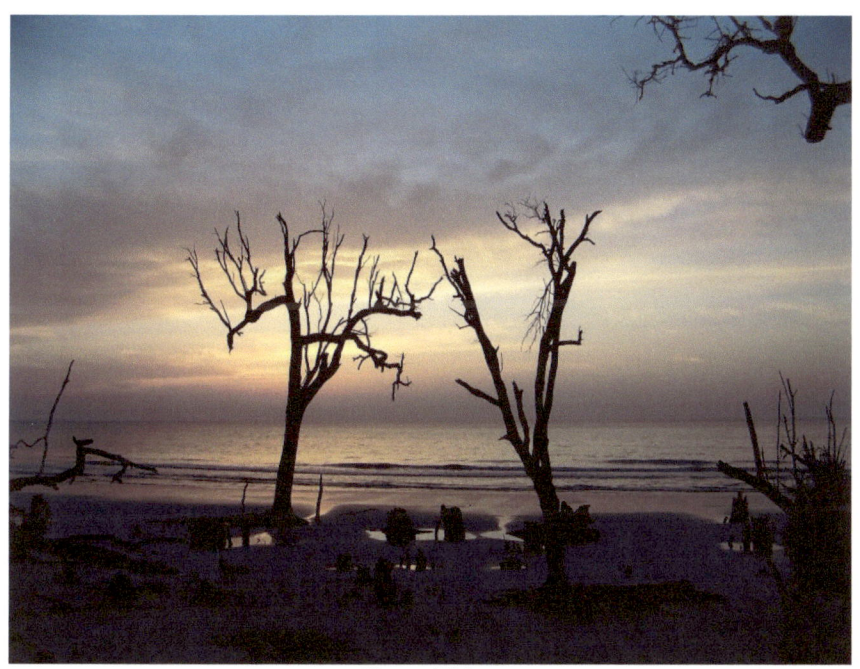

Shore Thing

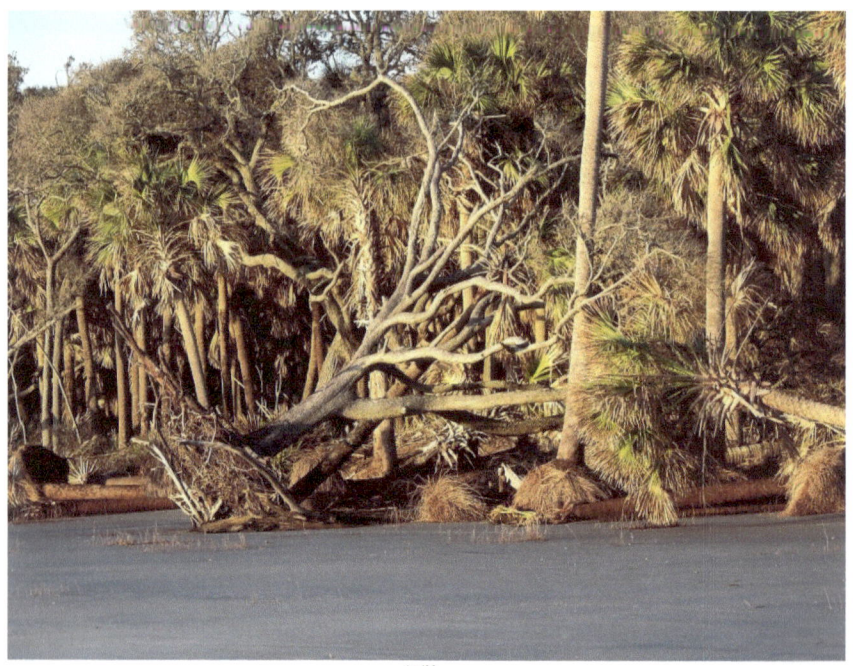

Tilt

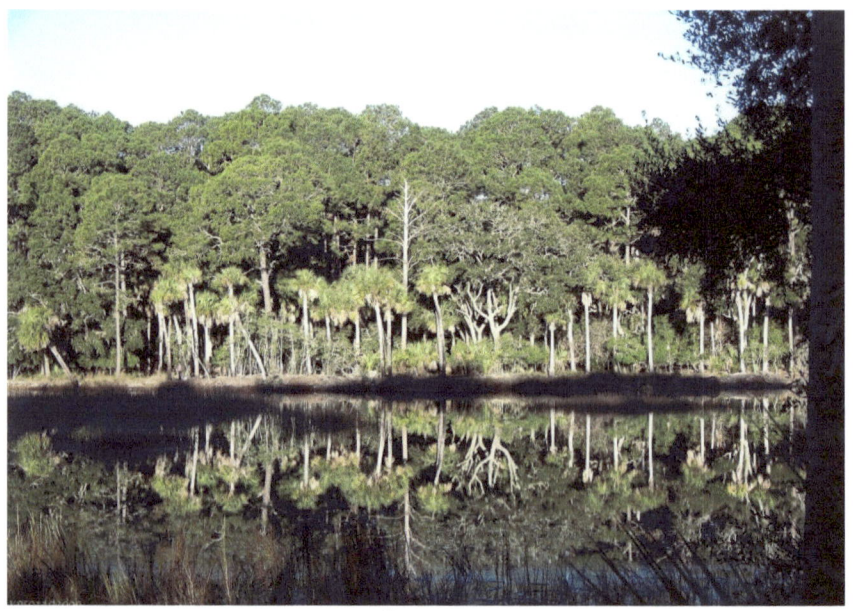

Lagoon

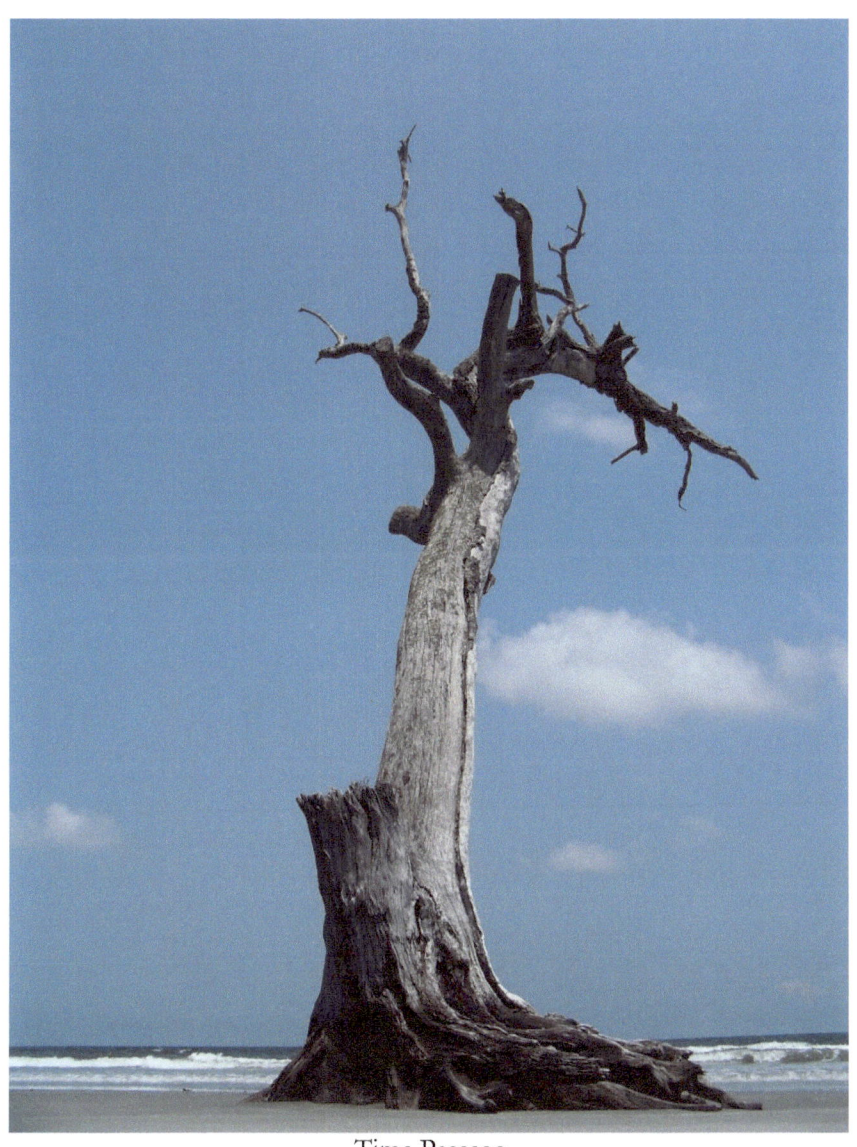

Time Passage

BOATS

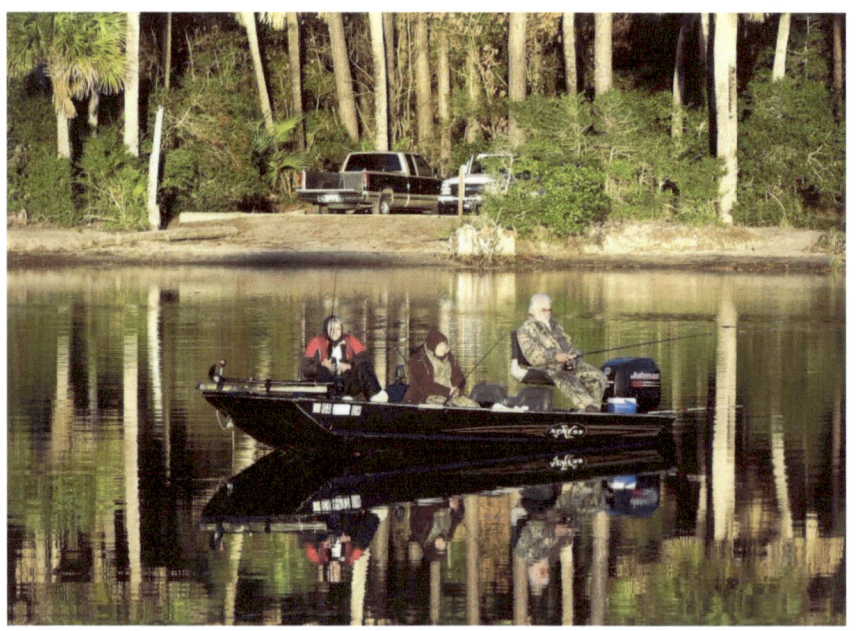

Dreamers

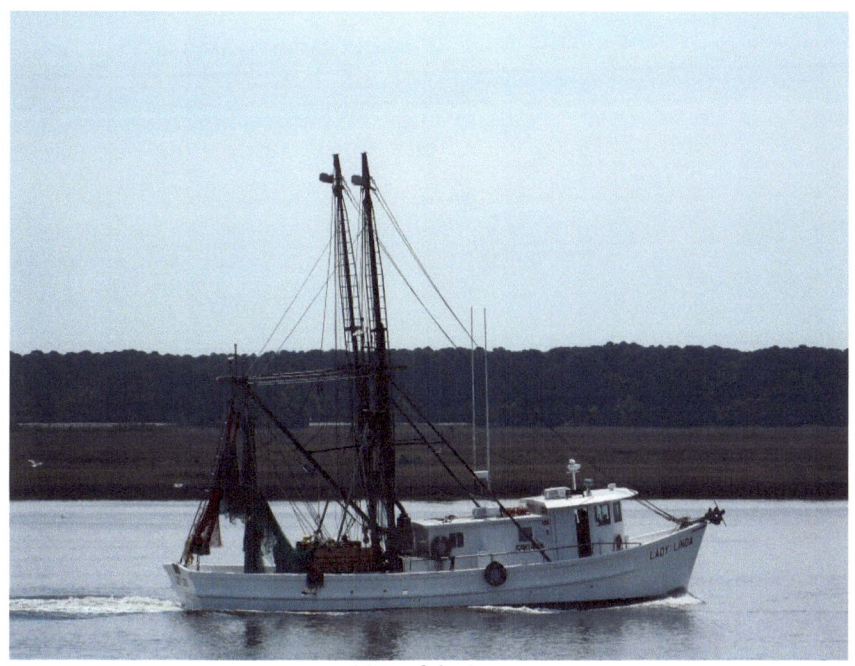

Hopeful Cast

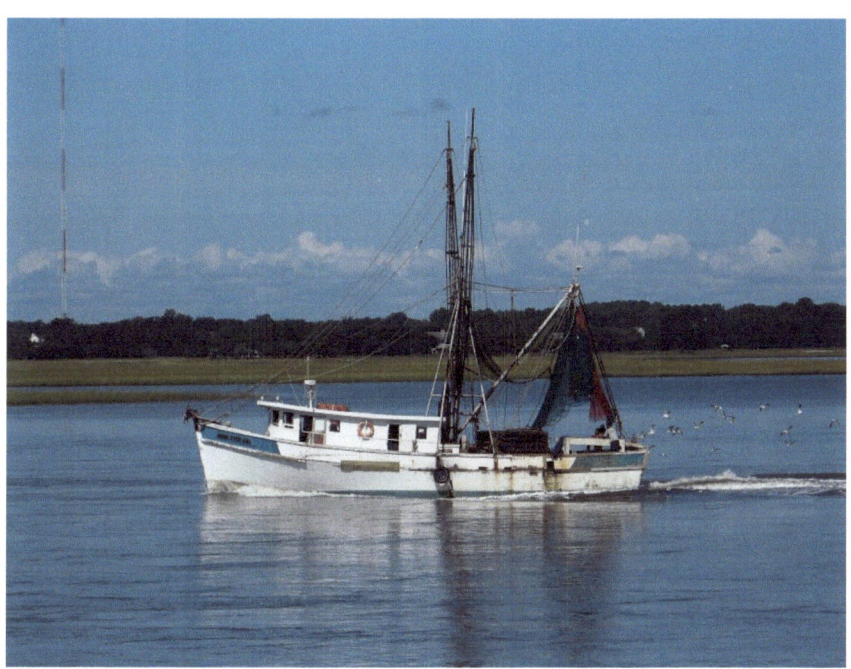

Ocean Yield

CRITTERS

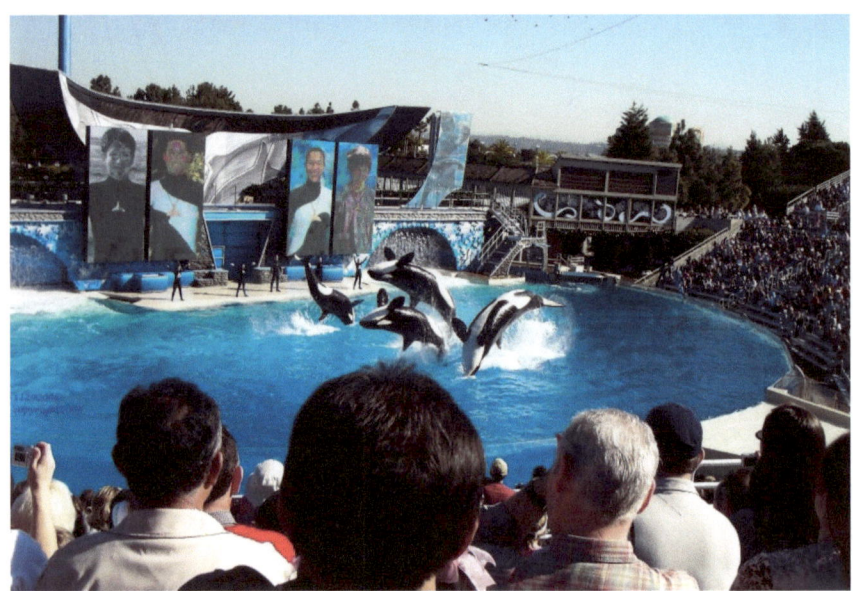

Flying 4

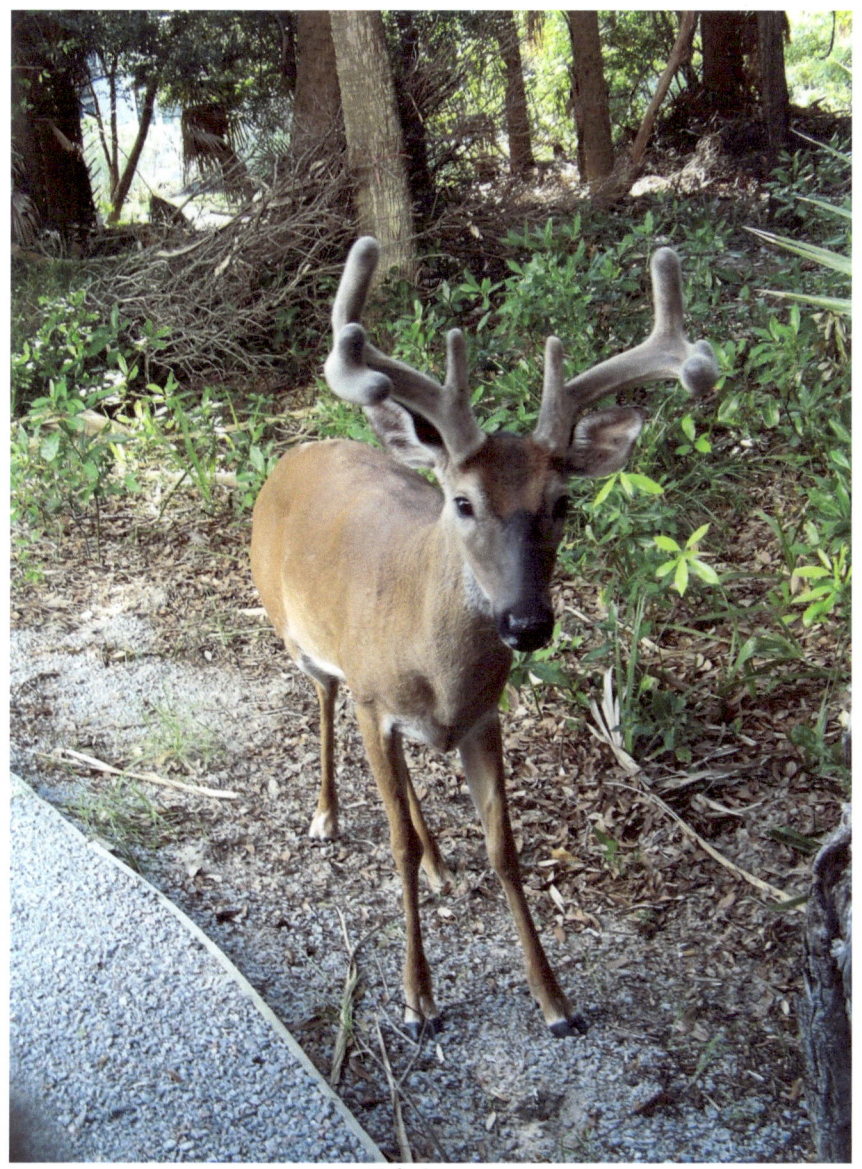

Felt Season

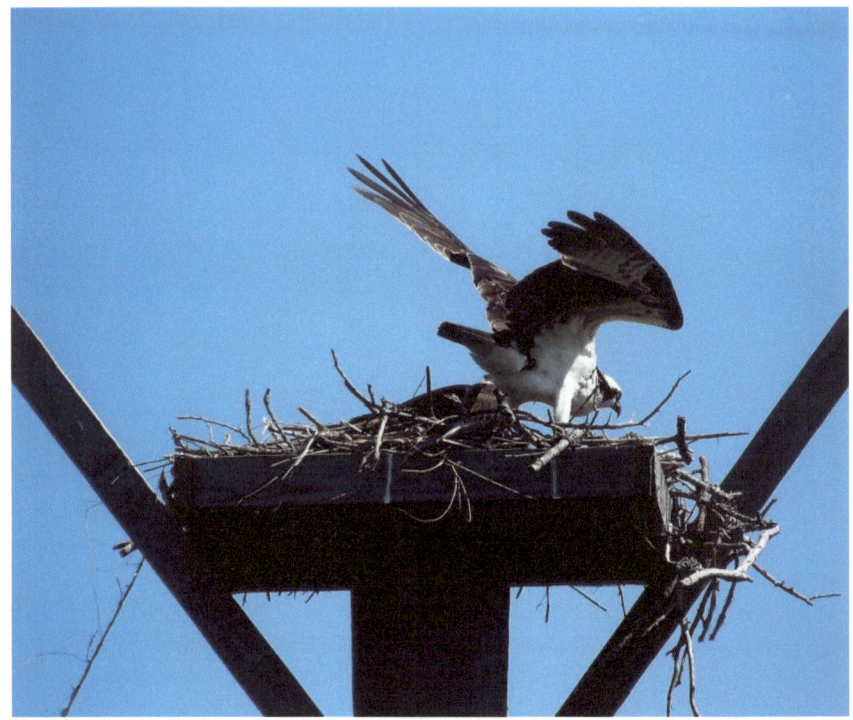

Fledgling

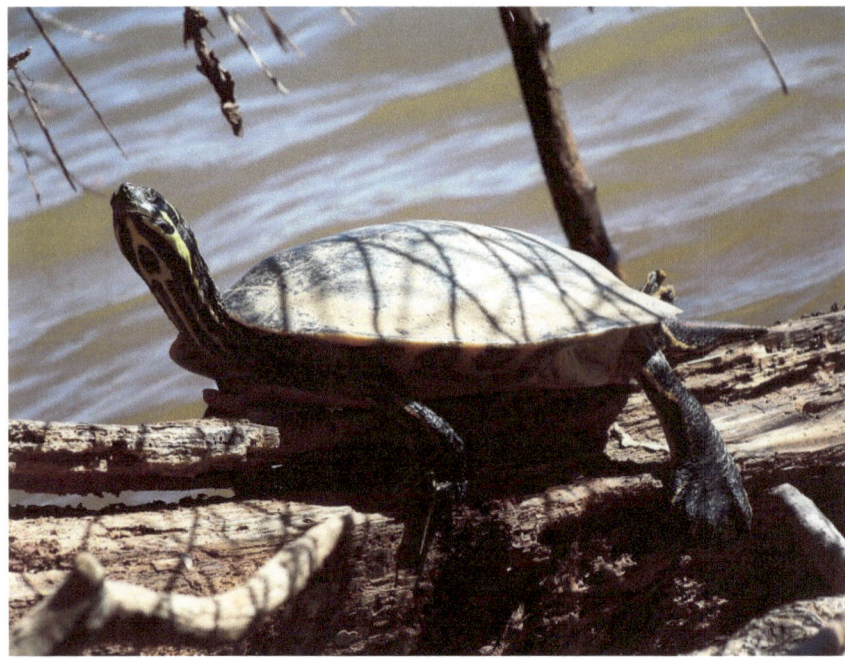

Logger

AUTHOR

Kevin has been an avid photographer since a young age. His artistic flair can be seen with his unique photos of driftwood and other offerings from the sea which he finds during beach combing excursions. Kevin does not retouch his photos. Preferring to keep them pure and natural as the items he photographs.

Rowmansea@Gmail.com
www.RowManSea.com

www.ingramcontent.com/pod-product-compliance
Lightning Source LLC
Chambersburg PA
CBHW041612180526
45159CB00002BC/825